Food for Thought

Food for Thought

Chris Husband

Christopher John Husband

Copyright © 2022 Chris Husband
All rights reserved.
ISBN: 9781739199708

Dedications

To all the food lovers around the world. I salute your gluttony and share your deep desire to say, "Oh go on then – one more can't hurt!".

To my wonderful wife, without whom I would surely have starved many years ago. You bring me love, joy and sustenance in equal measures.

To everyone who strives to be kind, considerate and look out for one another.

To the hard-working NHS staff who do a brilliant job in an ever trying world.

To those who are struggling with their mental health, feeling isolated and lonely. Be sure you have a purpose, and somebody loves you (I do, even though we may never have met).

And finally, to all the humans owned by cats. You know who is in charge – and it isn't you!

Be nice – it's the least we can do for each other.

Chris H.

Michelin Stars - not for me!

I have no truck
With fancy-pants muck
And multi-starred acclaim.
Is snail porridge your dream?
Or bacon ice cream?
Then we are not the same.
To see a quenelle
Is my kind of hell
Just serve me one big blob.
Amuse-bouche my ass
I think I will pass
Just shove it in my gob.
I don't want a jus
Just some grub I can chew
And it's gravy I do beg.
The only swish smear
On my plate should appear
When I dip my chip in my egg.
I do wonder why
There's no longer a pie
With pastry as thick as my head
What the hell's a pithivier
You can give them away

And bring me a pork pie instead.
So, no nouvelle cuisine
Or cordon-bleu that I've seen
It makes me want to gag.
Just some straightforward grub
That I get down the pub
With my leftovers put in a bag.

(This poem features in the online magazine "Scran" 1st Edition – October 2022)

Chippy Tea

Just finished work this evening
Now what to eat, let's see
Only one more day till weekend so
It must be Chippy Tea!
Chippy Tea
Chippy Tea
That's what it must be!
Chippy Tea
Chippy Tea
That's the one for me!
Now what grub do I fancy?
Fish, chips and mushy peas?
Steak pudding with lots of gravy?
Beef burger with lots of cheese?
Chippy Tea
Chippy Tea
That's what it must be!
Chippy Tea
Chippy Tea
That's the one for me!

Jumbo sausage, such a favourite
Curry sauce and lots of scraps
Meat pies that burn your lips off
Steak and kidney pie perhaps?
Chippy Tea
Chippy Tea
That's what it must be!
Chippy Tea
Chippy Tea
That's the one for me!
I might plump for fried chicken,
But that tends to be dry
That's it! A massive pile of chips
Topped with meat 'n tata pie!
Chippy Tea
Chippy Tea
That's what it must be!
Chippy Tea
Chippy Tea
That's the one for me!

Is Soup a Drink?

Is soup a drink?
Well what do you think?
Do you eat it from a bowl?
With some artisan bread roll?
Do you pour into a cup?
A great big mug to sup?
I admit I'm on the fence
And it's making me quite tense.
You see I do like both
Depending on the broth.
If a spoon will be required
A dish would be desired.
If the bisque appears thin
Then a cup it should be in.
A crust is fine to dip
When the soup's too hot to sip.
If it's thick enough to spread
On a slice of wholemeal bread.
Then that should just tell you
It's not a soup, it's stew!

Cereal Killer

DI Brunch followed the clues.
She could see the trail, crumb by crumb.
The vessel was empty, save remnants of a white liquid
surrounded by charred, bread-like dust.
The tablecloth was smeared with a greasy substance
and traces of glutinous red matter dripped from a discarded knife.
The sweet odour of seared flesh hung in the air,
pervading Brunch's nostrils and making her both gag
and feel hunger.
Pungent steam percolated the atmosphere as she
staggered out of the room.
"What's the matter boss?" asked DS Frühstück,
on secondment from the Landespolizei.
"You look like you have seen ein Geist"
"Worse than that Hans!" gasped Brunch
"I think we have stumbled upon a cereal killer!"

Eating Al Desko

Ham and cheese for lunch once more
My choice, I think, has become a bore.
Washed down with tea in my usual cup
I think I need to change it up.
Maybe bring a chicken leg
Or even peel a hard-boiled egg
A juicy steak with leaves beneath
But that gets stuck between my teeth.
Some feta cheese on pitta bread
Then shut my eyes,
Dream of the Med.
A glass of wine or maybe two
No, no there's too much work to do
Some crisps flavoured with Worcester sauce
Then crunch away like a great big horse.
A chunky Kit-Kat and some Irn Bru
The fizzy pop might make me spew.
It would be great to sit outdoors
But British rain just pours and pours.
I'd love to dine outside, Al Fresco
But will have to make do with Al Desko.

1, 2, 3, Banana

One banana
Two banana
Three banana
One more makes it Four
One step
Two step
Three step
On the floor
One slip
Two slip
Three slip
Crash into the door
One crack
Two crack
Three crack
Ow! My head is sore

Get on with it

I put my foot down with a firm hand
Let's call it a day
Before this gets out of hand.
"Whoa, easy does it," you said.
"Cut me some slack"
Well it's not rocket science, I replied,
You need to get your act together
Before we miss the boat!
"This is getting all bent out of shape!"
"You seem to want the best of both worlds",
"We don't want to be cutting any corners".
OK, let's not beat around the bush.
We are going to have to bite the bullet
Or we're headed for a perfect storm,
But we'll cross that bridge when we come to it.
"Let's not add insult to injury".
"We don't want to go on a wild goose chase".
We just have to hang in there.
Good things come to those who wait.
It ain't over till the fat lady sings.
"It's going to cost and arm and a leg"
"And I think you're skating on thin ice"
"I think we should take a rain check".
If we do that there will be a snowball effect,

We just have to weather the storm.
So shape up or ship out!
"That's the last straw"
"I'm going to hit the sack"
"The ball's in your court now".
"I hope you go down in flames".

Imbibition

escape their lairs soon after dark
to spill some claret, make their mark
sup straight from decanter neck
no will to keep desire in check
nocturnal wake
with ache
to take
a thirst to slake

Strictly Android

The robots danced the Bossa Nova
Whilst trying not to topple over.
Then they tried the Cha-Cha-Cha.
That didn't get them very far.
Their creaky joints could not survive
Any attempt to dance the Jive.
Their moving parts got very hot
With every step of the Foxtrot.
The American Smooth just didn't work
Especially when they tried to Twerk.
Performing tricky Tango spins
Just left them with dents in their shins.
The sensual Samba went with a clang
When the main drive shaft went with a bang.
Their Viennese Waltz simply fell flat
As drying gears screamed like a cat.
There was one dance that hit the spot
And that, of course, was the Robot!

Outsider Syndrome

Never feel part of the team?
Do you think everyone is ignoring you?
Is the current zeitgeist zeitgone for you?
Then you are suffering from Outsider Syndrome.
Is your voice echoing back at you like an empty hall?
Feel like you don't fit in?
Fed up with waiting for that affirmation that never arrives?
Then you are suffering from Outsider Syndrome.
Are you:
Too smart
Too dumb
Too old
Too young
Too quiet
Too loud
Too Good
Not good enough

All of these things point to you having what is known in the right circles (which of course you aren't in) as Outsider Syndrome.

If you would like help with this affliction, then talk to one of our specially trained support team. Just call 01NOBODYCARES and we may even confirm what you already knew?

What've you got to lose?

*callers may have something to lose, and your call may be ignored

Change the World - Maybe?

I might not change the world
but I might change my mind
which might change my life
then I might change your mind
and you might change your life
then you might change
someone else's mind
which might change their life
then they might change another's mind
which might change their life..............
before you know it
the world has changed

Urgent Care

Urgent care was busy
The sick were half in masks
The overworked and understaffed
Diligently performed their tasks
The patients patiently played patience
To pass the time away
Nurses nursing lukewarm drinks,
The first ones of the day.
Settle in for the long haul
The tests will take a while
Results will be pronounced professionally
Beneath the mask a sympathetic smile.
Broken bones are bound up
Slings slung around the shoulders
Notes taken, reviewed and signed
Returned to dog-eared folders.
No let-up in the intake
Staff begging for a lull
12 hours and counting down but
The waiting room's still full.
A changing of the guard now
Brings a modicum of relief
A chance to recharge the batteries
Escape the constant grief
But soon it's right back at it

Like they've never been away
Dedicated to this thankless job
For woefully inadequate pay.

The Appointment

Today I rang my doctor,
I thought I'd take a chance,
To book a new appointment
Very much in advance.
You see I am quite well now,
No aches or pains or gout.
But just in case I fall ill
Then there will be no doubt,
That I can get the treatment
My ailments will require,
I won't be left at A and E
Waiting to expire.
So a very nice young lady
Checked for open slots.
She joyfully exclaimed to me
There's lots and lots and lots.
If I don't mind some waiting
She'll fit me in just fine,
And I can see my medic
At twenty-five past nine.
"Today?" I asked astonished.
That, I didn't anticipate.
"No, No" she said quite sternly
September 2028.
I nearly snapped her hand off

Food for Thought

That date will bring me cheer
You see I'm scheduled to retire
That very same year.
With my appointment in my pocket
I can safely catch my chills
And because I won't be paying
I'll get piles and piles of pills.

Once Again

As I stand and gaze upon your grave
And remark on how your fight was brave
I remember souls can never die
They dissolve their form to sea and sky
Their presence sure as we press on
Safe in the knowledge they are not gone
But simply deferred to another place
Where we will surely know their grace
Once again

Put Another Way

Whilst we ignore the pachyderm in our living space
And enumerate our unborn ovum
There may be a precipitation of pets,
But let's return to the artists easel
And not go after untamed wildfowl.
It is futile to become lachrymose over discarded bovine secretions
For, enacting Satan's proponent,
I can't help but feel that when the deep-fried potatoes are depressed
We will ascend like a mythical bird from the detritus of flames
Glow like a heavenly body.
For each cumulus surely has an inner hoary coating.

Charlie's Dreams

Charlie loved to sleep all day,
All warm and cosy in his bed.
With a great big smile, he'd dream away,
Waking briefly to be fed.
Oh what adventures he would find
Whilst tucked up in his cot!
The birds that he would sneak behind.
The wild mouse captures he would plot.
Charlie liked to have great fun
With Ted the dog next door.
Along the neighbour's wall he'd run
So Ted would bark some more.
He'd stroll inside the grocer's shop
Getting under people's feet.
Then jump up on the counter top
And steal a tasty treat.
Hiding from the milkman
He'd jump out and make him scream.
Milk bottles would fall out from the van
And Charlie would lick the cream.
Charlie would find the warmest spot
Upon his human's knee.
But when he was getting far too hot
He would shade under a tree.
The thing that Charlie likes the most

As any cat's human knows,
Is to be tucked up, warm as toast
In a lovely, dreamy doze.

Conflicting Feelings

My world fell in when you fell out of it.
You tore me apart just as I thought it was all coming together.
I sank so low when you left me high and dry.
You had all the answers, but you just left me with questions.
Arriving, just as you left me,
Empty,
Full of grief,
Lost in a crowd of loneliness.

Sometimes

Sometimes life is very small
Sometimes it's not there at all
Sometimes it can be corrupt
Sometimes the end is quite abrupt
Sometimes it moves along just fine
Sometimes it improves like fine wine
Sometimes it just disappoints
Sometimes it wears away your joints
Sometimes it seems to take too long
Sometimes it's just plain wrong
Sometimes we wish it all away
Sometimes we beg for one more day
Sometimes it gives just what we need
Sometimes it takes and makes us bleed
When down to the final throw
Would we want another go?

THAT SHOULD BE ME!

I heard him on the radio
Interviewing some famous guy
Chatting to a Tik-Tok star
It makes me want to cry
You see I think there's something wrong
As I try to eat my tea
I get an overwhelming urge to shout
THAT SHOULD BE ME!
I recognised his dulcet tones
Unmistakably East Lancs
Softened just a little bit
Whilst in the Southern ranks
He's something of a celeb today
A local lad done well
But his success just grates on me
And makes me jealous as hell
You see I knew him before his star
Was in our atmosphere
When he was just a local hack
Pounding the streets round here

We shared a common starting point
To write about the news
But now I shop at TK Maxx
Whilst he wears Gucci shoes
He hob-nobs with the biggest names
Sports stars and politicians
The most excitement I can get
Is a trip to the opticians.
He writes the most fanciful stuff
Of buses on the moon
Whilst I sit and watch This Morning
And kip in the afternoon
He even had a game show
And the One Show gave him space.
My only effort in that way is
Shouting answers at The Chase
I know I could try harder
Maybe study for a degree
But every time I hear his voice
I think - THAT SHOULD BE ME!

Betrayal of Senses

I could see that you refused to deny it
your eyes betrayed your soul
the aroma of your disloyalty
formed an acrid taste in my mouth
the touch of your falsity
fizzed and popped in my ears

I think my soul is missing

I think my soul is missing
Sad times don't make me cry
At all my family funerals
No tears came to my eye.
The thing that touches a nerve for me
And stirs lachrymose unbound
Is something so benign and twee
No reason can be found.
To see another's emotions
Cracked voice, quivering lip
Brings some Pavlovian response
And from my eyes they slip
Drip
Drip
Drip

The End (for now)

Notes on the Author

Chris Husband is an author and poet, who has previously published a collection of poems entitled "Chips for Tea and other 10 minute Tweets" on Amazon.

Other published and soon to be published works are as follows:

- **Season's Janitor** – a poem for Autumn published on The Wombwell Rainbow (thewombwellrainbow.com)
- **Michelin Stars – Not For Me** – published in the Scran online magazine – October 2022
- **My Magical Bearded Friend** – a children's picture book – to be released December 2022
- **Good Morning Mr. Magpie** – a children's picture book – to be released November 2022

www.ingramcontent.com/pod-product-compliance
Lightning Source LLC
Chambersburg PA
CBHW040242130526
44590CB00049B/4224